Migration Ballads

A Poet's Journey

To Adam, Carolina, and their sweet daughter, with the friendship of Poetry.

Ali F. Bilir

ali f. bilir

pril.24, 2017
Tallahassee

Ali F. Bilir

Translated from Turkish by M. Ali Sulutas
Edited in English by Susan Bright

Plain View Press
P. O. 42255
Austin, TX 78704

plainviewpress.net
sb@plainviewpress.net
1-512-441-2452

Cover photo front and back by Mustafa Eser, Turkey.

Plain View Press wishes to thank Defne Bilir, Kuzey Bilir, M. Ali
Sulutas, R. Bruce Bickley, Jr, and Megan Anne Bright for helping us
get these beautiful words in English and Turkish presented in good
form.

This book has been made possible by the TEDA Project of the
Republic of Turkey Ministry of Culture, for which we are most
grateful and honored.

Contents

I
Migration Ballads

Poetry

I might have written
passionate lines
as if dying,
God lent his hand
letting fall
the magic of language
from his tongue.

I might have written
poems of my suffering
people, an image
pungent with carnation
and sweat.

Where am I now?

The poem: a word
melts the ice
on my tongue.

December '94

Cyclamen

My grandmother's swing
sways on and on
in the arms of death.
We travel to the utmost
edge of the coast —

A flower
cool to the touch,
as the mountainous cliff.

A sailor's lantern
does not light the way.
Does it shine?
Does death wait
until morning?

Is the lust of Kerem*
quenched; does it
penetrate the rocks
with his love?
A pink cyclamen
heats his flesh
with the burning health
of Asli.

March '95

* Kerem and Asli were lovers, one Muslim, one Christian whose
tragic love story is a favorite subject of traveling minstrels, Asiklar ,
meaning those who are in love.

Nomad's Migration Ballad

To my mother

Children,
sleepy woods,
sleepy beating heart,
a soul reflecting the rosy
hue of morning,
we must all leave one day.
Who can wait?

Awakening one morning
we'll find on our eyelids
the cold of dawn
chilled by a rose colored
breeze.

Children,
we are carried in an open bed truck,
exposed, wounded hearts bleeding,
autumn flowers in deserted hollows.
Cold are our hands
during the end-of-summer migration.
We are searching
for childhood paths behind us
now.

We leave behind
the never ending storm,
mossy rocks waiting
for ruins,
and our naked souls.

Continued

The storm hears
its own voice in the fierce,
howling wind,
among harvested vineyards,
at deserted hearths.

It penetrates the mountain
chill, a brand new day,
sun breaking out,
floating on the streams of a dream —
endless time,
the rosy hue of the morning.

Cultivated were the fields of dreams
every day, poppies would bloom
again and again.
The Milky Way hibernated
in dahlias —
a bluish vapor
used to brighten our darkest
nights.

From a point,
amidst the deathly hush
of great owls
we looked towards
the ocean-green of peanuts,
sesame and rice fields,
cotton candy clouds in the valley,
the warm breath of
factory smoke-stacks.

Clapping, joy rising up,
from this point
we looked to the future,

endless, woven by water
and light, suspended in city
windows, we were like a bird
with a timid heart.

Stretching ahead was
the country road beneath
our bare feet
wrapped in a mountain
breeze.

Our father ahead
always whistling, urged us
to keep walking, prodding
our lives, the tip
of a stick of broken hope
in his hand.

Ah, when did our sorrows blossom?
When did our father grow his beard?

Like stones thrown down Yousif's Well,
we waited for the season of moss,
with holy books not written yet
in our faithful hands,
raised by a lullaby, rich
with spell-binding words already
written,
such was our sorrow.

Our mother
holding Jacob's hand,
wrapping around her tiny waist
the kiss of the dessert sands,
the hopes of citizens buried in towns.

Continued

We didn't know yet
what anger was,
while we waited for morning,
bizarre it was.
For whom did our mother cry
on the path of the winding road.

Years later
before sunset reflected
on stone walls
collapsed at the threshold,
before evenings
our mother held a tiny pale
dream in her calloused hands
smelling of bread.

She washed and rubbed
every one of the passing days
spotlessly clean,
hung them over the branches of
the brand new rising morning.
She used to dry handfuls of narcissus
in the sunlight, carried hope
to distant stars —
wearing a white corn-flower
in her dreamland.

Sleep was like death in our eyes,
waiting for the morning,
the smell of home,
willow colored water running
bitter, drying up
just before reaching the sea.

The last day
with her usual voice calling life,
muttering, she said,
"This camel one day will
fall prostrate at the threshold
of every dwelling place!"

Our mother finished her ballad this way
never again to awaken.

December '94

Color of Death

Listen to
the wind blow
billowing, heated by fire
stirred up by Death
approaching, the rap rap
of darkness
gathering clamor
like a beating heart.

Fallen, drunken trees
curtains pulled across the sun,
autumn gasps sweeping time
with a ballad of snow-scented wind.

Can you hear the sorrow
that a mother hides in her chest
like an unwritten letter
that will sentence her son
to military service, to a death
tied to the broken wing of a bird?

Even a thrown stone
cannot penetrate the hidden
color of death!

                Gülnar, December '94

Sand Lily

Well-rested
the blue dreamy sea
heaps fine sand
onto a naked beach,
white pebbles
awaiting the lovely heat of
many Augusts.

Soon evening appears
with its mottled weaving
spreading clouds
over mountains
blowing wind
from burned-out places.

This sand lily tells best the passion
whirling around in my mind,
a drop of water fallen onto the desert.

September '94

Silencing Sound

Scabbed quickly
pain and sorrow
fill the calluses
of the heart
burning there,
silencing the sound.

The Great Horn

Is the ticking
of a smiling clock
the heartbeat
of time
alas, the blowing one day
of Israfil*
through the Great Horn,
his moldy breath?

* According to the Hadith, Israfil is the Angel responsible for
signaling the coming of Judgment Day by blowing a horn and
sending out a Blast of Truth. It translates to Hebrew as Raphael.
The blowing of the trumpet is described in many places in the
Qur'an. It is said that the first blow will destroy everything [Qur'an
69:13], while the second blow will bring all human beings back to
life again [Qur'an 36:51].

The 68'ers

We used to set fires
on mountains where
the heart of cities are today.

Extinguished are the shepherds' fires.
Blowing in the winds are
their fresh ashes.

Now,
I push my love
amidst passionate embraces
into a cave
on a deserted mountain.

Years Later, Istanbul

Such joy here —
the smell of naphthalene
when a chest is opened,
fragrant mornings,
my face, quiet, relaxed,
the dark shadows of
horse-chestnuts.

      Istanbul, 23.07.94

Lament

Night
covering the mountain,
the cliffs of the city
flow silently, secretly, nakedly,
on its winding path.

A storm
from which desert fire
comes secretly,
awakens the night
with passionate kisses,
with bird nests
decimated.

Ah, my burning heart. . .
My ravished country,
I wish I could sleep
one day silently at your knees.

Ah, pain. . .
Sharpen your blade even sharper.

July '94

Love and Death

Come inside my heart
in the valleys,
up to the mountain tops,
you, bare-footed love
that I kiss silently.

Enough.
Bare your sword,
Death, brother of pain,
pierce my deepest soul.

Embrace my body
lovingly.

June '94

A Child

Racing through vineyards
the child throws a stone
as far as he is able
searching for a remote God.

In an immaculate shirt
of pigeon wings
the child searches for
the whitest white
in the petals of a
mountain-ash blossom.

Gülnar, June '94

The First Time I Saw the Sea

Mother, wrapped in rags,
swinging in a hammock
rocked me to sleep,
singing lullabies
beneath a cedar tree until

I ran down stony paths,
hoisting on my shoulders
the past and the future,
hope and sorrow.

I still remember
how I cried for joy
the first time I saw the sea,
kissed the clouds
as I rode along
in a blue-bodied truck.

I have kept inside me
for many years
that sea,
it's salty tears.

June '94

The Road

To Defne and Kuzey

Passionately rivet
your attention
on life swaying
just at the brink of the cliff.

Wear across your hearts
the affection
you plucked from many fires,
many encounters.

Walk again and again
on this deserted road.

January '94

Rain Birds

I remember,
as I again traverse
the ancient city
I walked
in my youth,
how these calm,
still streets after rain
soothed
my uncontainable spirit.

I walked and walked
all night long.
Even Kafka, I suspect,
loved those old days,
the blurred, shadowed houses.

Years later,
I wear an Algerian violet
on my lapel,
search for my own
pale face at the cinema
as the rain birds
pass through my
imagination.

November '93

Goat's Thorn Flower

While sleeping
under the juniper trees
with their dense leaves
I adorned myself with
the long hair
of time—
a purple-colored, silky flower.

While sitting
under the dark shadows
of junipers
my soul
insulated itself
like a baby hedgehog
waiting for the growing hair of time.

Scot's Common Broom

Ah,
trembles my sleepy voice.
Venus shivers with cold,
while my face
kisses the cold night.

What if
I crosshatch myself
with yellow flowers,
a common broom,
washed in the chill dawn
and then,
discover myself?

Caper*

The word wets my lips.
The flower arouses my hopes
as it hangs down
amid thorny branches,
a white pigeon
from the tower of
a ruined fortress,
flowing through a dark era,
a foamy green waterfall,
caper.

Sitting at my knees,
at the edge of my heart,
a small, quiet child
looks towards blue
distant islands,
an eternal melancholy
narrated by
tales of a thousand and one nights
reflected like rose hues in his eyes.

*(Capparis spinosa L.) is a perennial spiny shrub that bears rounded, fleshy leaves and big white to pinkish-white flowers. A caper is also the pickled bud of this plant.

The Song Of Earth

When ploughshare touches
the arable land
awakening the body,
it embraces tenderly
seed scattered on the land.

Time scented incense
descends in the silence
of the night.
A child's shadow grows
in our souls—
its rain-wet hair.

While the warm hand
of the Sun reaps
the harvest of an open heart,
the curse of hard labor
infuses the song of
the fertilized soil.

1995

Love Of Taurus

I love
the terraced feet
of these Taurus Mountains,
the golden hair
of the sun
kissing these shores,
the streaming mane
of a white horse on the peak.
I love the Taurus Mountains
like a baby dripping in fluid
embraces life.

As Yunus*

Covered with ashes
so many words
since the creation of the universe
burning my tongue, burning my tongue.

Exhausted,
so many passions
since the creation of the universe
beating my heart, beating my heart.

Extinguished,
so many lights
since the creation of the universe
searching my hands, searching my hands.

February '94

* Yunus Emre, who lived 1238-1320, was a Turkish poet and Sufi mystic.

Smiling

This is how we smile
when we smile
from the window of a groping darkness
to the future
to better days for our country.

Who is not here
in this assembly of friends?
On one side, Ugur Mumcu,
like a rock.
On the other,
Asim Bezirci, Behçet Aysan,
Metin Altiok, Ugur Kaynar,
with their child-like smiles.

Ah friends,
the doves are fluttering.
Everyone is here
smiling whole-heartedly.

Autumn

Autumn returned
to the night.
Its shadow spread out.
Its pain fell on a stone
from the past.

Autumn returned
my heart
from the pain,
wove a poem and then
Autumn returned
again.

August '93

Holding Flowers

Whirling are the young girls,
wrapped in rage and grief,
singing softly love songs
of Asik Veysel and Pir Sultan.

A wind-song carries them away.
The children of Sivas are
holding flowers on the wings
of a purple butterfly.

Whirling are the young girls
burdened by love and hate.
Clouded by dust is the
bitter, smoky steppe
of Sivas.

Wounds of fire on their backs,
holding flowers
on the wings
of a purple butterfly,
the children of Sivas.

July '93

Don't Cry My Heart

To all the 37 great men
thrown into the black fire in Sivas*

Don' t cry.
Don't ever cry, my heart.
Time is raiding
the dead of night
while your lily-white hair floats
in the water.

Don't cry my heart
while fire falls into the night.
Here is life,
spun at the point of love.

July '93

* 37 poets, authors, dancers and intellectuals who died in a fire on July 2nd, 1993 at Hotel Madimak, where they came to stay for a cultural activity in the city of Sivas, known as the birth place of Pir Sultan and Asik Veysel, who were humanist minstrels in Turkey.

Hero

*To Ugur Mumcu**

In the Taurus Mountains
in Anatolia,
my Turcoman mother
composes a ballad,
weaves carpet without pile.

Every olive tree
cries out with the strain
of a thousand years
of making the earth green.

A flower-crowned heart of Cybele,
the mother goddess,
embroiders dreams of life
like a star,
gliding through the night sky.

My Turcoman mother
composes songs
to the heather
all the way at the top
of the majestic mountains
that love may grow.

Continued

She scorches her own heart
with a burst of pain
for every broken olive branch.

My Turcoman mother
composes a dirge
after every brave young man is killed.

February '93

* Ugur Mumcu (August 22, 1942 - January 24, 1993) was a Turkish intellectual, investigative journalist and columnist. He was killed on January 24, 1993.

The Date Of Birth Carries a Mortal Scent

Death
bleeds the night before daylight.
The master does his duty.
Neither a noise or a sound,
only mound of wet earth
remains behind,
a note on the calendar,
scribbled a date:
the date of birth carries a mortal scent.

A dark-leafed shadow
covers the table of a poet.
An ink pot tipped over,
deep well, labeled:
Parker Ink — black,
and a reed pen
with its sharp teeth,
a sharp knife,
a reed broken long ago,
a drop of blood,
scribbled a date:
the date of birth carries a mortal scent.

Migrant Bird

Ah,
you yellow leaf migrant bird,
you pass by
singing ballads,
ride on the feathered wings
of a poem.

You pleasant flower, migrant bird,
you fly over my head every day
wafting love
over the mountains.
The seas belong to you.

One day stop here,
please, migrant bird,
rest a moment,
chat with us.

September '92

Five-Finger Mountains

Kyrenia's flower-decorated hills
that I hold
in my kite-flying,
child-like heart,
my tiny hands
dyed with henna,
her Five-Finger Mountains
smile at the sun.

Wave your hands,
and colorful handkerchiefs
to departing lovers.

Wish them good luck
to join their beloved ones.

Kyrenia, 7 July '92

Beautiful Bird

Stretch out your wings
my beautiful bird,
fly away with my spirit
share with me your joy.

While my heart is beating
take me away to the sea
wherever you wish
over the mountains, to the forests.

Let the tip of your wings
touch the blue sky.
Let us linger all day long, then set
me down on a deserted island.

Adana, 6 July '92

Spinning Wheel

Death!
Is it a red-hot cinder?
Is it a fire embracing the night,
the faint sound of a spinning wheel
clacking continually?

Spinning wheel
clacking continually?
  clackedeeclack
  clackedeeclack

Hey!
hovering purple flower
stained by the blood of Jesus,
faint sound of a spinning wheel
driving the silent night,
spinning wheel
clacking continually!
  clackedeeclack
  clackedeeclack

Taurus Evenings

*To Osman Sahin**

During harvest,
on the fresh cut fields
those lonely Taurus evenings
with my father,

we ate potatoes embedded in ash
pulled out of the fire
with a tiny stick of hornbeam.

We dipped them in salt.
I even liked the night owl.

No one knows now.
I cannot tell anyone.

Even unto death,
I can not speak of it.

I ought to go there again,
to that grass-covered
wind-blown terrain
where my father is buried.

Adana, June '92

*Osman Sahin is a Turkish short story writer.

Kissing

Kissing
thin lines of my dreams
drawn on my forehead
by my faith

Kissing
sprouts turning green
in an ocean of green,
daisies,
poppies,
ant hills,
purple crocus,
anything scented,
opening
into the day
kissing them all.

The Ballad Of Homer

Never have I seen
in all my life
his indigo colored sea,
deep purple, salt white,
dripping off my eyelashes.

Never
in all of my life
at night have I seen
or heard the silent ballad
of Homer cross the pale
silvery face of the moon.

While a pale gray horse
glided out silently
from the tip of a cane-pipe,
my broken heart waited
and the walls of Troy collapsed
where an unbridled wooden horse
was grazing.

                    1992

Maybe One Day

Passion reminds me
with longing
all those writers
and their art:
Joyce, Faulkner, Rilke…
Portrait Of An Artist As A Young Man
Dying In My Bed
Brigge's Notes…

Ah, *Ulysses*,
the dream of time immortal,
a legendary emerald bird
on my mind.

Possibly one day
the spoiled child in me,
forgotten for sometime,
will wake up.

Perhaps,
overshadowed
by the silver moon,
the woman at my window
awaits nightfall,
eagerly.

I Used to Hang Out and Pick Up Dreams

Bending and twisting
the reddish sandalwood tree
and my own dry skin,
the wind wove my dreams
into the falling leaves, and so
I used to hang out
and pick up dreams
all day long.

My mother listened
those long days
to tales of creation,
touched the grayish beard
of my father
with her fingers
dyed with henna.

I waited, snug in my
corner of the world,
fascinated by a cloud,
like a god
eating itself.

I dreamed
and wove dreams
all day long.

                    Gülnar, May '92

Before Nightfall

To Saadet, my wife

I must go away again
before the nightfall
sinks into my heart,
before I am disheartened.

We used to warm
the whole world,
like a small bird,
in our hands.
We used to feed
all the flowers we picked
by kissing time all day long.

Now, who would run after
a tired stream?
Youth disappeared long ago
without leaving a trace,
sunk into life, an eddy
alongside a willow shaded road.

May '92

The Ages

Cold, cruel night
sleeps in me.

Lullaby:
Sleep not my child.
Open your eyes.

B.C. — A.D.
The age of the atom, media,
turns into a black beetle.
A bug with time for a shell,
pushes, rolling away
the world, pushes cruelly,
gun barrel, avalanche, storms.

Ahead are the world's children
in the elbow of a sling.

Gülnar, February '92

My Grandmother's Story

The sky wept all day long
for my grandmother,
standing like a child on tiptoe,
in sorrow and loneliness.

The subtle face of nightfall,
descended, always silent, while
my rose-scented grandmother
waited at the window.

It is not easy to tell,
my grandmother's story,
which began the day
she was left a widow.

Question

Crossing at a gallop
the narrow bridge to heaven,
have you asked God
the source of all this sorrow?

And did God reply:
Here is a beautiful world
for you, sharper than a sword
famine, war, love
use it to your liking?

March '92

Snowdrop Flower

One day,
on a snow covered mountain
I saw a refugee child, shivering,
a snow drop flower.

She hung her head
like a dying poppy,
nestled under the shade
of a cloud.

Her eyes lit the night,
like fire-flies
cleared of sorrow
by the dark waters
of the Euphrates.

On a snow covered mountain
I saw a small child —
narcissus flower.

Time passes,
seeking miracles.

1991

Your Loneliness

A forgotten poem
is your loneliness waiting
on the cross of bitterness
in the unknown language
of death.

Lost time
is your loneliness
swimming in blood red wine.

Exile
is your loneliness
buried in Middle Eastern deserts.

Is it Moses,
or is it Jesus,
or is it Mohammed
always gathering
your loneliness?

A Letter From Someone In Exile

*To Orhan Selim**

White clouds,
hanging down
from the sky,
please tell my mother
I'm terribly homesick
and on my tongue
is the bitter salty taste of
a bewildering land.

In a country
cold and dark
an exiled heart
waits in a frame of iron.

November '90

*Famous Turkish poet Nazim Hikmet who used the pen name of Orhan Selim.

II
Autumn Memories

Autumn Memories

Autumn,
time to collect
late summer vines of dried peppers
from the earthen roof-tops of huts,
in rushing rain,
black damsons, sliced apples,
melancholy around us,
amber bunches of grapes
that pale in boiling ash water.

Dried passions
gradually lean across the day,
from a shadowed-faced sky,
are bagged up, taken away,
along with an urgent desire to arrive
at last.

Anticipating the next migration,
we moderate our worries.
Life settles back,
to the ancient riverbed
and we remember only traces
of bitter sorrows
which end quickly,
like summer, like life.

Autumn
is this bunch of sweet basil
I hold in my palm
like a faded photograph
that appeared suddenly
and was wiped clean
by time.

Continued

Autumn,
at night, as moonlight
flows down from my window
your smell lingers on my flesh
along with ancient memories
as we wander far from home
together again.

Silk Handkerchief

Short is the human story,
incomplete the whistler's song.

Death is a gift
we beg of fortune.
At the height of the day
it springs up at the front door.

Life may be short,
but it is a very long road,
resembling a just-born butterfly
which becomes itself.

Possibly
it is our childhood
we hide in our breast pocket —
the scent of a silk handkerchief.

At the Threshold

Until darkness sets in
the beloved
listens for a footstep —
the return of the distant traveler.

Only a falling star
slides to the doorstep.
And the heart gathers up
its broken longing.

Fearsome Game

I pick up thrown stones
instead of roses. At dawn I walk
over broken glass to the gallows
barefoot, heartbroken
but forthright, without bowing.

Do not avert your glance
from my passion.
My quivering body is witness
to the fear. It is a long walk
I know. The cinders beneath my feet
are burning, they are the soil.
I wear a shirt of fire.
Let your attention water my voice.

I am picking up thrown stones
instead of hope. Constantly bleeding
is my heart. I wish my vessel of sorrow
were full. I wish I walked in the garden
of words like Pir Sultan.*

I have been picking up these thrown stones
since Spartacus.**
Every love is an Ebabil.***
Bad words are like bullets.
I am again crucified.

My only life is with you
in the past. To escape this fear
the whistle of memory trills on.
Sorrow's poison cannot kill,
hope is born of you.
Oh! My heart carry me!

Continued

* *Pir Sultan Abdal*: A 16th Century revolutionary poet; leader of the rebellions against the unjust, oppressive and cruel Sultan of that era. He was arrested, stoned and later hung by the Ottoman Governor Hizir Pasha. While he was stoned, one of his loved friends was throwing him roses instead of stones. He was offended nevertheless. Two verses of his poem he wrote relate to this event: "Dropping down over my head like the rain / Most hurting me are the roses thrown on me by my best friend."

** *Spartacus*: The revolutionary and fearless leader of the first slave uprising in history happened in the Roman Empire. He was captured in the year of 71BC by the Roman General Pompeus and later executed.

*** *Ebabil*: A bird resembling a swallow as mentioned in the *Holy Koran*. Legend says that these birds, carrying stones with their beaks, were sent over the soldiers of Ebrehe, the tyrant Governor of Yemen and the entire army of the Governor was killed by stones dropped down by the birds.

Purified Soul

Naked, the soul is purified.
With each laugh
the sleeping mind blinks.
The road, the heavy burden
and distance make love linger.

A joyful soul is purified
of terror.
Passion is not greedy
on smiling lips
waiting to be kissed.

Leaving,
the soul is purified
for its final adventure.
Death only has meaning
for those left behind.

Passing Through the Steppe

It is a vast steppe and
the night is frozen, icing
down my window silently.

It is snowing on the past,
no breaks.

Neither the Mediterranean
nor the sky, small as a palm
in my memory, remain.

Junction after junction,
cross-roads, all roads
vanish as I pass
through the steppe.

Taurus Field Is In My Hands

It's a new journey to the past,
free of the heavy burdens of today
and the worry.

It's a miniscule equation
pulling the core of my heart.

It's a tranquil autumn morning
while a new morning is blooming
far distant, like death,
from my birthplace.

The Taurus Mountains
are in my hands, blackthorn
cutting my skin, childhood memories,
my gallnut bag hung over
the old oak tree, the tiny water wheel
I made from red pine bark,
and set in the stream to make
an imaginary mill.

My neighing purebred Arab horse
is a willow branch
between my tiny legs.
I ride with
childhood dreams
in my saddle,
all set to follow the road
wherever my feathery heart
takes me.

Wondering Child

Whenever I anticipate
a journey
a familiar feeling,
distance too vast,
springs to mind

and I carry
with me
the night,
the fear of loss.

Migrant is the child
from this mountain town.
Loaded on his shoulders
by birth
are his burdens.

My Father By the Well

On the roads of the migrant,
my father, drawing water from
the well with his hat, patched,
held in his hands hope
for the rising morning.

If the cloud of destitution
hadn't existed,
would his hair have grayed
so early, might he have
turned around,
seen the birds?

Migratory Birds

Wherever I go,
searching for my voice
through a field of sunflowers,
I pass gravel-dirty roads.

At the end of each summer
migratory birds
return in smaller numbers.

Sundown

Sound rattles wrongly.
Closed is a door,
a window,
no one listening to
its loneliness.

Sun descends suddenly
over the deserted steppe.
A train passes by.
I am riding it
through the night
just talking to myself.

On all their voyages
migrating birds
carry their own hopes.

The Voice Of Darkness

Listen to the voice of darkness
to the verses you whisper to the night,
your farewell, the prelude of the morning.

Listen to the voice of darkness,
a timid nomadic boy in town
bundled in his loneliness.

Listen to the voice of darkness,
the broken heart
pumping hope through isolation.

Violet Scented Night

Year: 1967
An autumn wanderer,
I ached for Istanbul
as I crossed through
the Straits of Gibraltar
in a small, worn-out fishing boat.

On a desert evening in Algeria,
I lay down on the sands
along the Mediterranean Sea
and counted falling stars
on my fingertips.

My God, how high was
the sky?
And Africa!

The night smells violet
whenever the isolation
in me is touched.

Penelope Abject

A bouquet of narcissus
for hopeless Penelope who
endures suffering
without expectation.

I walk the whole day
with no break to catch breath.
In my heart
a poem of love and resistance.

I smoke a cigarette,
offer bitter tea
to the workers on strike
as we pass shoulder to shoulder
through Kizilay Square in Ankara.

Narcissus are in season.
I ought to buy a bouquet of narcissus
on my way back to Mersin.

Ankara, March, '96

Reminiscences

Whenever I remember
the town of my childhood
the shiver of palm trees,
my hands are wounded
by the imaginary thorns
of oranges.

No matter how close I get,
that is the distance I am
from myself.

I understand finally
whoever has the void within,
must drop himself
down through the emptiness.

Cemre*

What can be said about life
except one must live fully
in the time given.

No one is a master driver.
Remember the living heath
gives warmth to air, water
and soil. The tadpole
drops it's tiny tail as soon
as early summer touches it.
A rotten walnut leaf
floats on the water.

What can be said about life
except one must live fully
and leave when the
time comes to go to
the other side of the stream.

Always we search
for a brand-new homeland.

*Translator' note:
The title of this poem in Turkish is 'Cemre', which is an Arabic
word, also used in Turkish as well, meaning a hypothetical warming
up of the air first, then the water and finally the earth in February.

Back To the Beginning

Deja vue,
back to my first step
towards the exit
of the labyrinth.

I am walking in the dark.
My eyes are covered
because I cling to the past.

I am not a reptile,
or a worm,
not the wing of a bird,
or the fin of a fish.

I am falling down.
Hold my hand.

Deja vue,
back to the beginning —
a bumpkin student
from the countryside,
in Istanbul, a soldier,
a weekend boarder,
on the ebony street
asking for the address
of a well known house
to tell friends, a memory
of flashy living
in Istanbul.

Really, when did we smile
at that old photographer
with our childish faces
that always hide something?

Continued

Deja vue,
I'm back at the beginning,
going back, seeing myself
in the photographs.

How Blue Is Istanbul

It's a familiar feeling,
forgetting while expanding,
the names of the flowers that I love.

I remember her most,
the girl with violet eyes,
but she is as distant
as Istanbul.

We are climbing, hand-in-hand,
to the Beyazit Tower
by the stone stairways,
whirling to the sky.
How blue is Istanbul?

Wise Is the Child

Wise is the child who
hears in its innermost world
the voice of the darkness
it was born in

who learns sorrow
from its mother
while waiting at home
for its father

love stirred to blood,
the relentless power struggles
of the grown-ups,

the child does not forget
the number of stars
that it touches
with the tip of its finger.

I Longed For My Childhood

I longed for my childhood
ground to flour
between two millstones
and vintage laughter.

Excessive, independent
stones nibbled my bare feet
as I traveled from here to there.
I left all this in the valley.

At every twinkle of the eye
poppy flower dreams disappear.

The Bitter Day

Mankind used to sleep
before blood dispersed
the butterflies of nature
over the bread to be shared.

The day bitterness set in
to the heart of Adam,
from Kabil to Habil,*
a dark destiny
that time never forgot
immediately began
to write its own diary
in its own yellow book.

* Cain and Able

A Child Recognizes Love

The day the baby is born
it closes its eyes
to hear its own voice.

Then loneliness sets in,
the cliff, the sea builds up
over its inner world
and swallows its loved ones.

When fire touches its small fingers
and the mother kisses burnt fingers,
the child recognizes love.

While Passing By

How many lives have passed
like this, how many breaths of windy
daylight, lifetimes of stories,
so many kinds of love, growing
old, disappearing without a sign?

You should write this, my heart
tells me, replying to the voice of the wind,
the faces in the rocks, as I rest
at the edge of the cliff
like a single grain of sand,
a salamander, the last trace
of a road that's changed.

I must write this.
While passing by Gülnar,
the Söğüt plateau, a nomad's house,
I was reproached by all that chance
brought to my mind. But it grew cold.
I wrapped myself in my own warmth
once again on a bright night full of stars.

My Hands Go To My Heart

I wish I had taken trips,
I say to myself, to unknown places,
that people were less strange to each other
than our own feelings.

I return to this familiar point
and feel, along the bank of the river,
wind sweeping away
all the footprints in the sand.

Whenever I read a poem
about separation,
my hands go to my heart.

Every Morning

Every morning
helplessly I look at
the face reflected in the mirror
how strange
how distant from myself.

I stand aghast:
this weary heart
the smile on my face.

Every morning
a fresh hope opens my door
when I step out to the street.

The Brand New Day

Good morning to the New Day,
the joy of life in me.
Good morning
to you Almond Tree
touching my window.

Good morning to you, Fresh Breeze,
Doorway, facing the sun.
Good morning, My Warm Home,
My Smoky Fireplace.

Good morning, Road to the Bazaar,
Street with Chirping Sparrows.
Good morning, Uncle riding on a bike,
My Villagers,
riding to the bazaar
on the fender of a tractor,
on the tailgate of a truck.

Good morning to you, Good Man
sharing bread
and love with me.

In a Diary

The love affair of a marble and a rose
is awash with robust feeling.
The aged flesh
bleeds with each kiss —
love entwined with death
in the yellowed page of a diary.

One petal falls after another
onto a marble forehead
with the rosebud skin of time
turning pale.

On the River Bank

Tell me where to stand,
here, on the river bank, how dark
and wet the road we walked.

Here,
at the threshold,
the key under the doormat remains.

Whenever a bird flies
overhead, I turn my face
toward the mountains.

Ispitiren Grapes

A bunch of Ispitiren grapes
hanging on the vine,
a glass of wine, refresh the body.

Passionate arms
embrace the darkest night
like a clinging, climbing vine.

At the threshold we watch
for passion coming with Dionysus
to harvest the grapes.

Intimate Questions

A child asks himself,
where God finds shelter
these winter days,
with whom does He play marbles,
does He cry behind His kite
when its string is broken?

A woman asks herself
why men fight with each other
instead of sharing bread.

A commander is not a mother
crying and mourning
for loved ones killed.

Poem For Marbles

Hey you,
child throwing stones up to the sky
and standing right underneath,
here are some marbles for you,
instead of candy.

See the sandcastles
you have built on the streets
of Baghdad.

I came all the way
from the other side of the ocean
to bring you these colorful
marbles, a gift from Santa Claus.

Come out when I say, *apple*,
You, child come out from your
shelter and let's play marbles together.

Nay Nay Ninay Nom!

I wish today were Bairam!*
  Nay nay ninay nom!
  Nanny-nanny boo-boo!

Why can't we live as we desire?
Why can't we live with our own dreams,
with bees, with butterflies around us,
and dappled lady birds
without greed, or quarrel, or money?
  Nay nay ninay nom!
  Nanny-nanny boo-boo!

Where are all those good old days of childhood?

I wish everyday were Bairam
  Nay nay ninay nom!
  Nanny-nanny boo-boo!

I wonder if I am insane—
  Nay nay ninay nom!
  Nanny-nanny boo-boo!

*Turkish, Islamic festival.

At the Edge Of Emptiness

At the edge of emptiness
is the smile of a child
hiding its wound.

What remains
from tiny hopes?

A letter with no address
searching everyday
for the right recipient.

Reflection From a Broken Mirror

Where should I write her name,
autumn scent, her touching hands?
In which language should I call out
the love that flies over her face,
a wave of swallows?

Perhaps it is our childhood
reflecting back
from a broken mirror.

The Shadow Behind Us

What would a man think
who has given up
then unexpectedly

searches for the hand of a friend,
a branch of a tree to hold on to
even as he dives into the emptiness?

Reminding us
we are each lonely,
the shadow behind us?

After Long Separation

Your house is still empty.
My heart is wounded.
In the den the sofa sits where
it always has. The day melts away
when I touch it.
A wild silence surrounds me,
weeps like a dirty cloud.
Your geraniums, your chrysanthemums shiver.
I bring them in from the balcony,
and all the flowers you loved.
The seasons are leaning on me.
I brew fresh tea, your favorite,
but your glass is empty
still on the table.

I listen to the foot steps
of the passing days
annoyed by even the shortest
separation.

A door is opening,
your smiling face falls
across the weary sofa
like a dried out leaf.

Your house is still empty.
Hope is bandaging its wound.

Don't Ever Worry

In the book written by life
all your dreams are carved
across the face of a stone.
All your adventures
are forgotten or mixed up.

Say, *Good Morning,*
to the smiling face of the day.
Keep the window open.
Water the flowers,
the sweet basil on the balcony,
as you know, the more care
the greener life grows.

If I suddenly pass away
one day
don't ever worry about me.

Rain and Child

Rain
silently opens the muddy road
of life. Squeezed
between wealth and scantiness
morning awakens
with a cool touch
inside the dream
of a freezing child.

Rain
is a traveler with no home.
Beneath clouds, wearing the cold
covers of darkness
on a tiny, straw legged night,
it is an unnvited guest on roofs
covered with zinc plates.

Hey, yoo-hoo!

Silence.

Human isolation
on the brink of a cliff
shivering for whatever reason,
traces the footsteps
of a wounded child.

Rain,
always a story of sorrow
in its own language,
a child, annoyed, escapes
wire bars, passes through
when it can —
hands smelling of oranges.

Continued

When love stirs
sun lightens the face —
just a few drops.

Lonely Heart

When I open the window
in the morning, already
the day is changing.

Waves of passion rush
through the tips of my fingers.

We search for the past,
usually on our faces.

Death lies in ambush
for our beloved ones.

Why is a bucket of water poured
after the departing traveler?

Cold is the face of the death
because it doesn't speak.

If one is too lonely,
a night watcher
will close your eyes.

Midwinter Flower

Going, coming,
going, coming, going and. . .

Between parallel lines
emptiness rests
like the midwinter flower
that goes and never arrives.

Life Is Better Today

The life is a little better today,
the voices of children
in spite of a smell from the distance.

Life is a little better today.
I am over fifty and grow
tranquil, as after a storm.

Life is a little better today.
We serve only olives and bread,
the happiness of a cup of tea.

Life is a little better today.
In the poems of Nazim, I search
for the longing of my father.

A Boy Named 'Baris'*

*To Sevgi Soysal***

Who had given
the name of 'Savas'
to this peaceful boy
who sells
crisp simit
at noon, in Yenisehir?

Which is why
Ankara smells like sesame
every morning at daybreak.

Alas, who wrote
with dark hands
the word 'savas'
on the forehead of this boy?

* 'Baris' (as read in Turkish, 'Barish') means 'peace', also a name of a boy; 'Savas' (as read in Turkish, 'Savash') means 'war', also a name of a boy; 'simit' is a ring-shaped bread-roll, sesame ring and smells like a 'simit'.

** Sevgi Soysal was a Turkish author who wrote a short story named "A Boy Named Baris".

A Dervish Of the Bektashi

To Umit Sariaslan*

Hiding his childhood,
the Fakili roads
full of dust and earth.
He dreams of Hittites
and the aromas of Ankara.

He is a Dervish of the Bektashi
with a ticket in his pocket,
and can never be bent by oppression.

Every time he smiles
a black locomotive comes and goes.

* Umit Sariaslan is a Turkish poet, writer, critic.

Closure

*For Cetin Altan**

The words of a wise man
fall down the eyelids of a dead bird,
are washed in tearful glances
remembered eventually as text
in small brackets.

Another day is over.
Passing by the upper market,
a boy carries under his arm
a loaf of bread the size of a bird.
His tired dreams are lost to wind,
to the waters of the river.

The face of a woman and a boy
are the world.

News from Hades, a wounded bat,
your eyes blind, no one should
hear this confession: *I couldn't see*
God, just my own naked self.
Besides, Where are you going?
The road is over here.

All you do is pour water
every day, buckets of water,
burial services for the dead.

To the wise man,
it is a long journey, tracing
someone's history, their voice
through long darkness.

*Cetin Altan is a Turkish journalist, author, critic.

Solve This Puzzle Friends

*To Ece Ayhan**

Our sea is deep, friends,
and salty, yours for tears.
An invisible hand
pulls you into the turbulent
undertow, down
to the sea floor,
if you are
a clumsy swimmer.

Our load is heavy, friends.
On our shoulders, from childhood
a mountain climb
and we're blindfolded.

Life is a blindfolded player
calling, *Home,*
on the first instant
we find joy.

We have a long way to go, friends.
Close your eyes and suddenly
the night swallows your light.

Life is a puzzle,
hides everything in itself,
starts and ends instantly.
So, solve this puzzle, my friends.

*Ece Ayhan was a Turkish poet.

Faces In the Photograph

*To Isa Celik**

A moment from the past,
fixed in the frame
of a photograph,
a silver story, held in time.

A miniscule narrative
hung on the wall,
where did it begin?
Where does it end?

Faces in the photograph
before sunset,
afterwards are changed,
but don't age.

*Isa Celik is a Turkish photographer and short story writer.

The Wise Man

To Nevit Kodalli＊

The old sage closed his eyes
the whole world, a sound
a lemon flower on his face
closed his eyes.
What does he hear?
The whole world is a passion,
a Yunus Emre in his voice .

Close your eyes.
Do you hear the old sage?

The Mediterranean Sea
is the whole world
and your heart is in your hands.

＊Prof. Dr. Nevit Kodalli is an internationally known musician and composer in Turkey. Some of his famous works such as *Ataturk Oratorio* and *Gılgamis* and *Van Gogh Opera* make him an essential figure in Turkish and World Music literature.

Verses Of Hattushili

*To Elif Akin**

You and the sun may go out
together. You can touch
the shoulders
of your friends,
the city that you live in
will not grow smaller
for your dreams.

We are sometimes fragile,
fall behind our loved ones,
keep careful secrets
on rainy days.

Perhaps a young university
girl finds a boyfriend.
Her vast hopes
are the wake, the shadow
of humanity's isolation,
fear and worry,
that trail behind everyone.

There are verses
of Hattushili, the wise man,
you carry accross
the deserted park
on rainy days,
the verses of Hattushili,
the wise man, King of Hittite,
who had seen better days,
who was a symbol of happiness,
the letter he wrote
to the Council of Nobles,

Continued

one to his grandson, Murshil,
these are to be read again,
a tale of passion engraved
on the surface of gliding time
blended with clay, water and fire,
the apple that ripens,
a worm inside,
the hope and sorrow that sleep
on an embroidered frame
of time.

Yes, the letter always comes back,
a stamp on the envelope,
Not at this address.
It falls among unopened envelopes
like an amber autumn leaf
mingling with all of our silences.

You may go out today
along with the sun.

*Elif Akın is a friend of Defne Bilir from Hacettepe University.

Prometheus and Sisyphus

*To Mehmet Atay**

The pain of separation
I repress
with tobacco.

A red-hot sun setting
over the waters of the Bosphorus
wraps the pain of Istanbul
around my heart.

I encountered a very few
wise men, as I searched
for my essential self
in the stories of Prometheus
and Sisyphus.

I was chained for
writing a poem of freedom.
I carried, without reluctance, hope
on the wings of words.

*Mehmet Atay is an editor and publisher in Turkey.

Prior To Long Journeys

To my daughter Defne

Looking back to my roots,
long journeys, many steps,
how gracefully my homeland
has run after me, snow covered
those glittering clouds
just above the changing mountains.

Like a small child am I
whose heart cannot match
the rhythm of this world.

The lonely wind has gone
with me. In me is desire, desire
such hope it brings!

Maybe I will fall into
the emptiness of my youth.
Quite alone is this home
with the door latched
and behind me the serenity
the emptiness
all my long journeys.

Translator Notes

by M. Ali Sulutas

Autumn Reminiscences (Autumn Memories)

Contemplated during and translated after an autumn grape harvesting and syrup making trip to Gülnar on 10.10.04, the home town of the poet and the interpreter. Interestingly enough, this first poem in the book has been translated as 'first-in-last-out', whereas, the last poem had been translated as 'last-in-first-out'. First drafted in Mersin at dawn, Sunday, 17.10.2004.

Silk Handkerchief

Translated on the lawns of the Blenheim Palace, where Winston Churchill of England was born in 1874, Woodstock, Oxfordshire, England, 16.06.04.

The Game of Fear (A Fearsome Game)

Pir Sultan Abdal is a well known Turkish poet of the 16th century and is the originator of the Alevi-Bektashi literature. In his poems, written and read with pure colloquial language, love of people, daily life of villagers, beauty and love of nature, humanism and mysticism are the main points.

Purified Soul

Translated on the lawns of St. James Park and the Green Park, during the intervals of leisurely city tours, and shopping, London, England, 15.06.04.

Passing Through the Steppe

Translated on a KLM night flight from Toronto to Istanbul via Amsterdam, over the vast steppe-like land of peaceful and industrious Canada, 24.09.04.

Taurus Field Is In My Hands

Contemplated on the morning of 30 May 2004 in the camp tent at the peak of the Lamas Canyon, during the annual tracking over the Taurus Mountains, and completed translation in somewhat deserted home town, Gülnar, Mersin, 10.10.04.

Wondering Child

Contemplated the translation during a journey to Toronto and Hamilton, Canada, and completed after an autumn excursion to the mountain town Gülnar, 11.10.04.

My Father By the Well

Translated by the "St. Paul's Well" in Tarsus, Mersin, Turkey, 11.09.04.

Migratory Birds

Translated on the backyard porch sitting on a deckchair after watering the lawn, trees, and flowers, and filling up the trough with water and the mangers with nuts and sunflower seeds for sparrows, woodpeckers, blue jays, cardinals, at the house of my dearest friends Prof. Virginia and husband Oktay Aksan, in earthly tranquility, Hamilton, Canada, 22.09.04.

Sundown

Translated on a bus, while traveling from Istanbul to Ankara, during sundown, in Lake Sapanca region, east of Istanbul, the Sea of Marmara, Turkey, 28.06.04.

The Voice of Darkness

Translated in Ottawa Train Station, under a dark sky, Canada, 31.03.04.

Violet Scented Night

Translated on a small plane with twin propeller, from London to Amsterdam with 44 passengers at 15,000 feet altitude, over the English Channel, 21.06.04.

Hopeless Penelope (Penelope Abject)

Translated on the slopes of Taurus Mountains, Mersin, during the breaks on a couple of hiking activities, next to the white-yellow, wild narcissus, Spring 2004.

Reminiscences

Translated in natural and beautiful Tallahassee, Florida,USA, 20.01.04.

The Vital Heath (Cemre)

Contemplated translation during the 'warming up' days of early Spring and drafted early Fall of 2004 on the Mediterranean coast, Southern Turkey, and re-drafted at the garden home of my two dearest friends Prof. Virginia and Oktay Aksan. The title of this poem in Turkish is 'Cemre', which is an Arabic word, also used inTurkish as well, meaning a hypothetical warming up of the air first, then the water and finally the earth in February. I initially had a difficulty to title this poem in English: I had come up with something like, 'Increase of warmth on earth', 'Warming-up of the earth'. Because it's an Arabic word, Oktay took out his Arabic-English dictionary and I picked the most suitable one among the meanings: It was nothing but 'The Vital Heath'. Moreover, Ginny has suggested me to use 'tadpole' instead of 'froggy', which may have been misinterpreted. Many thanks for their more 'vital' assistance. Hamilton, Canada, 22.09.04.

Back To the Beginning

Translated at Atatürk Airport in Istanbul while waiting several
hours for the flight to Miami, and onwards to Tallahassee, Florida, to
meet Defne and Salih,14.01.04.

How Blue Is Istanbul

Translated on aircraft from Amsterdam to Istanbul, on the way back
from Miami, over the Black Sea towards Istanbul, while descending
Atatürk Airport, 25.01.04.

Wise Is the Child

Translated in Hyde Park, in front of the pond, a Spanish girl
at 2.5 years of age, with her parents, was very active, cute, the
Marlborough Gate, 20.06.04.

I Longed For My Childhood

Translated during the annual 'Children's Day' activities, Silifke,
23.04.04.

The Day Bitterness Sets In

Translated in Woodstock, during a visit to Blenheim Palace, Oxford,
16.06.04.

A Child Recognizes Love

Translated during the annual 'Children's Day' activities, Silifke,
23.04.04.

While Passing By

Translated on a night flight from Montreal to Amsterdam, over the
Atlantic, under the bright stars at 30,000 feet, 70/80 Celsius outside,
31.03/01.04.04.

My Hands Go To My Heart

Translated on a KLM flight # 671, Amsterdam to Montreal at about 30,000 feet over the Maritime Provinces of Canada, the Atlantic Ocean, Monday, 22.03.04.

Every Morning

Translated at the hotel room in International Miami Airport, in the morning after missing my flight to Amsterdam/Istanbul last evening, due to a late connecting flight, and just before going on a much desired Miami city tour, 24.01.04.

The Brand New Day

Translated at the Schiphol Airport, Amsterdam, on my way to Montreal, 22.03.04.

In A Diary

Translated at London City Airport, on my way back after a 10-day visit, 21.06.04.

On the River Bank

Translated at the hotel room in New Orleans, on the bank of the Mississippi River, on a week-end holiday, which was my dream, a treat of Defne and Salih, 18.01.04.

Intimate Questions

Translated during a visit to Defne and Salih, the daughter and son-in-law of the poet, Ali F. Bilir, in the natural and beautiful Tallahassee, Florida, US, 20.01.04.

Nay Nay Ninay Nom!..

Translated during the only Bairam in the world for children, which was established in 1920 by Ataturk, the founder of the modern Turkish nation, and was declared by the UNICEF in 1979, as the 'International Children's Day' to be celebrated in a joyful, colorful international festive fashion on 23rd April. Silifke, 23.04.04.

At the Edge Of Emptiness

Contemplated at the residence of Ottawa YM-WCA, during the children's session by the swimming pool, and translated later in the hotel room, Canada, 26.03.04.

Reflection From a Broken Mirror

Translated at the residence of YM-WCA, in front of a broken mirror, 26.03.04.

Don't Ever Worry

Drafted the translation in a setting of stones, rocks, flowers, plants, trees, greens, birds, dropping waters, newly weds photographing, children playing, grannies waiting, the beautiful Botanical Rock Garden, Hamilton, Ont., Canada, 18.09.04.

Rain and Child

Translated on KLM flight # 627, from Amsterdam to Miami, at about 30,000 feet altitude over the Atlantic Ocean, somewhere between the Greenland and Canada, outside temperature was -70C degrees, wonder of clouds, 14.01.04.

Life Is Better Today

The residence of Ottawa YM-WCA, east view, at 05:30 when
the remaining city lights were dancing with the rising brand new
glittering daybreak lights, 26.03.04.

A Boy Named 'Baris'

Contemplated during the first 'World Peace Day Festivities', while
most of the children were feeding themselves with 'simit', around
the 'Ismet Inönü'-Winston Churchill Peace Park', established in
1993, Yenice, Tarsus, Mersin, 01.09.04.

A Dervish Of the Bektashi

Translated on a commuting train from London Victoria Train
Station to Gatwick to catch a ride to Chartwell, Westerham, the
Sevenoaks District, to visit the old museum house of the legendary
Winston Spencer Churchill, England, 18.06.04.

Faces In the Photograph

Inspired for translation after meeting the photographer Isa Celik in
Gülnar and Mersin on a photography taking excursion along the
coastal region, 02.05.04.

Verses of Hattushili

The preliminary translation was completed on a KLM flight from
Montreal via Amsterdam to Istanbul, over the snow covered
Balkans, 01.04.04 (not April fool).

Prometheus and Sisyphus

The rough draft translation was completed in Istanbul Atatürk
Airport while waiting for the time to fly with KLM via Amsterdam
to Montreal, 22.03.04.

Prior To Long Journeys

Started translation at dawn while listening to the music of Rodrigo's 'Concierto de Aranjuez', completed at mid-morning while listening to the music of the late Baris Manço's 'Journey at Sight'. In fact, this was the beginning of the translation of the book, on a (LIFO) basis. Interestingly enough, I happened to translate the first poem in book as the last one (FILO) basis. Mersin, 10.01.04.

Epilogue

Poets have neither a home, nor a town, nor a country.

Their real places are the mountains, the rocks, the valleys, the trees, the swings, the kites. As you will see, Ali F. Bilir is standing up on his tasseled kites and/or magic carpets and flying around among the wondering stars.

Similarly, the translators have no permanent dwellings either. Therefore, I managed only to temporarily hitch a ride on the magic carpet of the poet. Hence, these harmonized translations of the poems have as much the same flavor as the original ones.

I practically took the book with me wherever I went, especially on long journeys. Surprisingly, I was able to spare time for translation. Therefore, this English version of the book carries the flavors and feelings of the peoples of those settings and environments.

Naturally, at times, I took the liberty of including a few words as footnotes to the poems to open up the window of the scenes where the contemplations and/or translations took place. I even put a few explanatory notes and definitions for visual imagination.

Considering the nature of the poems, I've included a sub-title to the English version: 'A Poet's Journey'. Furthermore, I've added to some poems new words or lines to enrich the spice and the flavor for the literature appetite of the English-speaking poets and poem-lovers.

Originally, it was my proposal to Ali F. Bilir to translate these poems into English. Although it was a very difficult task for me to comprehend the depth of the meanings of the verses and to transform them into another language, English that is, I happily took on the task. I am glad that I did. I was lucky, because I had been through a path of the life similar to the life of the poet, some years earlier than he.

Therefore, in some respect, I found myself in these poems. As I have been living in North America since 1968, I felt obliged to share the aroma and the flavor of the poems reflecting the feelings and the state of mind of a poet, a native of the country of Turkey.

At times, especially when facing difficulties, human beings want to go back to their days of childhood. I don't know about you, but I personally, like the poet, I wish I were in my childhood days when the autumn comes our way with its colorful leaves falling down around our heads. I am grateful to Ali for bringing back the nostalgic feelings of those good old days.

May I take this opportunity to express my gratitude to Dr. Bruce Bickley for his rewarding support and guidance in this diligent work of translation. Upon reviewing my file of translation of 'Migration Ballad', the first poetry book of the poet, Professor Bickley has encouraged me sincerely. As a result, this book has come out our way.

My sincere thanks go to my honorary niece Defne, the darling daughter of Ali F. Bilir, and to his beloved wife and moral support, educator and writer F. Saadet Bilir. Dearest Defne has initiated this cooperation between us for the publication of the poems in North America.

M. Ali Sulutas

About the Author

Photo by Monika Kuki

Ali F. Bilir was born in 1945 in Gülnar, Mersin, Turkey. He attended the School of Medicine for a year, but graduated from the Faculty of Pharmacy, University of Istanbul, in 1969. During his university years, he worked part-time at a tourist youth hostel in Istanbul as a reception clerk and later as a manager. In 1967, as an adventure, he toured Europe and North Africa, mainly on foot. For a while, he lived in Essex and London, England to improve his English, working on various jobs such as picking fruit from trees, washing dishes and serving as a waiter at restaurants. He participated in the student and youth movements of 1968.

His poems, short stories and articles on various subjects have been published in local, regional, national, and international periodicals, magazines, and journals. His work has won many awards: *Günes Magazine*,1990, Sweden, fiction award; 1993 *Orhan Kemal*, 1993, fiction award; *Ibrahim Yildiz* - Honorable Mention for the book of *Göç Türküsü* (*Migration Ballads*), 1996, poetry award; *Samim Kocagöz*, 1998, fiction award; *S. Avni Olez* , 2004, Jury Special Prize for the poetry book of *Güz Animsamalari* (*Autumn Reminiscences*).

His published books in Turkish are: *Usüyen Sicak Düslerim (My Shivering Warm Dreams)* (Stories), *Göç Türküsü (Migration Ballad)* (Poems), *Elestiriden Günceye (From Critique to Diary)* (Critiques and Diaries)*, and *Güz Animsamalari (Autumn Reminiscences)* (Poems), *Mersin'de Aydın Olmak (Being an Intellectual in Mersin)* (Compilation) [co-compiler: Orhan Ozdemir], *Orta Asya'dan Toroslar'a Gülnar (Gülnar – From Central Asia to Taurus Mountains)* (Research: Language, Culture, Social Life) [co-author: F. Saadet Bilir].

E-mail: alibilirf@hotmail.com

Printed in the United States
116716LV00001B/49/P

9 781891 386398